Fill the Seat

THE
Onboarding
Blueprint
FOR YOUR
Nonprofit Board
Chair

Dr. Kate Shilvock

Kate Shilvock
Fill the Seat / Kate Shilvock —1st ed.

Paperback: 978-1-956989-40-3
Hardcover: 978-1-956989-39-7

To my husband Matthew, my son Colin, and my daughter Eleanor. Lucky me to be with you.

Contents

PART 1:

The Problem

CHAPTER 1

It's That Time Again...

As a nonprofit leader, you're likely familiar with the frustration of filling the board chair position. Endless cycles of succession characterize the governing structure of nonprofit organizations. The reasoning behind short term limits is to prevent stagnancy, integrate fresh new ideas, and protect the organization from the long-term consequences of an incongruous board chair. This is great in theory, but the translation to practice gets tricky. One of the biggest challenges with this ongoing turnover is simply finding a willing and able person to fill the board chair position. In fact, many studies (including my own) show that it's the rare nonprofit that can easily fill the board chair position. Most chairs volunteer because, well, no one else would. Once the position has been filled, the challenge becomes ensuring the new chair is properly trained and up to snuff. Research indicates that many small- and medium-sized nonprofits think they lack the resources to provide effective onboarding to their board chairs. However, when done well (or even done at all!), onboarding is much less resource-intensive than you might think and can easily become a part of your culture.

Oh, but then there's the fact that you've likely got your hands full with managing your teams, fundraising, operational challenges, governance issues, communications, etc. Finding the time to prepare a new individual to assume this position may feel daunting, especially when you know they won't be sticking around long. BUT, dedicating effort to onboarding is incredibly important. Why? Think about it like this. The governing structure of nonprofits is unique in that every time term limits are reached, you're tasked with finding and hiring a new board chair. That new chair, who could be someone who never served on the board, may have zero nonprofit experience, and is only qualified based on their willingness to volunteer, *that person* then becomes your boss. That's right, your boss. You'd be hard-pressed to think of any other setting where this is common practice. In the nonprofit world, it's standard operating procedure.

Executive directors are often so overwhelmed with their own job of, you know, running an entire organization, that the thought of onboarding a new chair seems daunting, at best. I know the idea of adding one more thing to your plate probably makes you cringe because I've been in your shoes. During my career supporting, mentoring, and being an executive director, there were times when my colleagues and I secretly hoped a new chair would just be able to figure everything out on their own. Really, we just crossed our fingers that the new chair wouldn't cause anything to implode. Other times, we prayed they wouldn't step in too heavily on the administrative side and into our world, that they will stay in their lane while we stayed in ours. Sadly, board chair turnover is a big, stinking pain in the you-know-what.

This book aims to significantly reduce the stress of board chair succession by helping you establish a simple, evidence-based onboarding system. Onboarding provides an opportunity for you to start the relationship with your board chair off on the right foot. Through onboarding, you can establish communication needs, review the responsibilities held by each of you, and set clear expectations for one another. When a chair is provided with the knowledge and support they need, they can do their job (... so you don't have to) and your relationship with them can blossom into a productive partnership that strengthens your nonprofit's culture and effectiveness.

Don't put this book down yet! I know what you're thinking: *Great, another thing to add to my already overwhelming to-do list.* As if you're not already flirting with burnout and struggling to balance your life. My goal isn't to load your plate up with more *stuff* to do. I want to help lessen your load, and proper chair onboarding can do just that. Yes, there will be a bit of upfront work, but I promise it will make your life much easier each time you have a new chair in the future (and even make the onerous process of identifying your next one smoother). I'm going to explain why chair onboarding is so important, what it should entail, and the most simple and efficient way to get it done.

In this book, I've compiled my professional experience, my research, and insights from board chairs to develop a comprehensive guide for tackling the onboarding dilemma. Keeping common challenges and limitations in mind, my goal was to create a short handbook packed with actionable strategies and advice. This book will help you develop an onboarding system that you can easily implement each time you're tasked with bringing on a new board chair. While the system may need tweaks as your organization evolves, this blueprint will greatly reduce the future stresses and burdens associated with onboarding, help alleviate common operational problems in the nonprofit sector, and strengthen your governance framework.

For the sake of simplicity (and efficiency), I've divided this book into two parts: The problem and the solution. It's hard to fix something if we don't fully understand how the problem came to be. We're first going to take a magnifying glass to the problems surrounding nonprofit board chair succession, from the perspectives of both the executive director and the board chair. Then, I'm going to tell you about my decades of experience in the nonprofit sector, as well as my research on chair onboarding (the latter is a lot more interesting than it may sound).

For those of you thinking, *Listen Kate, I don't have all day here*, I hear you! Part 2 of the book is focused on the solutions to the problems I outline in Part 1.

Each solution is organized into a chapter that has practical and actionable strategies that will help you develop your onboarding blueprint. Additionally, several helpful PDFs and templates can be downloaded for free on my website to be used and shared with others, www.centricnonprofitconsulting.com.

Alright, let's begin.

CHAPTER 2

The Board Chair – Why it's a Hard Seat to Fill

Research indicates that around 90% of individuals who hold board chair positions at nonprofits are only doing it because nobody else volunteered. Yep, not a typo. Whether it was due to a lack of volunteers or unexpected departures, the decision to assume leadership responsibilities were sometimes reluctantly accepted by participants in my research. "I took on the board chair role out of necessity," admitted one board chair I interviewed, highlighting a pragmatic attitude that's common among board chairs who weren't skipping with excitement at the prospect of assuming the position. Another (among many sharing similar thoughts) told me, "Nobody was doing it so I said fine, I will, but I didn't want it." The dismal reality is that very few people *want* to be a board chair. This can be particularly frustrating for board members and executive directors who, in compliance with [sometimes ridiculously] short term limits for board chairs, are tasked with recruiting new people to fill the role almost as soon as a new chair takes over! While I believe chair onboarding can drastically improve an individual's willingness to volunteer, it's important to first look at why this role has gotten such a bad rap.

For starters, the pay stinks. And by *stinks,* I mean there is no pay. Naturally, the time commitment for a board chair is greater than that of board members because it is a leadership role, but the unknown of exactly how time-consuming the position will be is often a deterrent. I've worked with board chairs who told me their volunteer time lands at about 5 hours per month…and others whose organizations require ten times that. The problem is a board chair won't know what awaits them until they take on the role, regardless of how transparent the organization is. With many board chairs working full-time jobs, running businesses, raising families, and trying to have some semblance of a life, those with many professional and personal responsibilities may be reluctant to add more to their plates.

The position can also be a hard sell because it may require dealing with significant conflict. Board chairs lead the board by engaging individual members to work as a unit. The job involves facilitating board meetings, showing strong leadership, and supporting and supervising the chief executive, all while following best governing practices. Because board members typically come from a wide range of backgrounds and experiences, chairs must navigate conflicting ideas and opinions within the board, as well.

In addition, the relationship between the board chair and executive director can be difficult and adversarial, with three out of four of these dyadic relationships being so antagonistic that one or both parties step down! Fundamental differences exist in the roles and responsibilities of the two positions. The board chair represents the board of directors and holds the ultimate authority and decision-making power within the organization. That's right, it's not a misprint. Legally, the board chair role (filled by a temporary volunteer) oversees a nonprofit. The executive director, on the other hand, is responsible for the day-to-day operations of the nonprofit (and everything that entails) and reports to their board of directors, which has the power to hire and fire them. Feeling the inherent tension of this relationship already? Sadly, it's an endemic aspect of nonprofit leadership, and one that I think causes executive directors to work *around* their board chairs rather than work *with* them.

Personality clashes, communication breakdowns, and power struggles can further exacerbate tensions between these key leaders. In some cases, board chairs may micromanage or overstep their boundaries, undermining the executive director's authority and autonomy. Conversely, executive directors may resist board chair interference and begin feeling undermined in their leadership roles. The success of a nonprofit ultimately depends on a constructive relationship between the board chair and executive director, but achieving this harmony requires clear communication, respect, and shared commitment to the organization's mission and goals. One of the most effective ways to achieve this harmony is through proper chair onboarding.

The challenges surrounding the board chair position are further compounded by term limits and rapid turnover. Board chair term limits are implemented to bring in fresh perspectives and prevent stagnation. However, this intentional renewal can sometimes lead to the loss of valuable expertise and institutional knowledge if there is no onboarding blueprint to preserve it. Frequent turnover can also create leadership vacuums that disrupt the continuity required for effective governance. For example, board chair turnover can create shifts in strategic priorities that generate confusion among staff, volunteers, and board members. And if the nonprofit's internal culture is off from the top-down, then it's pretty much a guarantee that your external community will feel it, as well!

Without onboarding, another significant deterrent to potential board chairs is that they're thrown into the deep end. Board chairs often have no experience leading within the mission-driven nuances of the nonprofit sector (or, leading at all). They usually receive insufficient guidance after taking the role, which is partly caused by little or no communication with previous chairs. I've found that board chairs are usually expected to learn their roles by osmosis, by just sitting in a meeting and watching what other board chairs do! In the rare instance when information *is* provided, new board chairs may feel like they're getting information thrown at them, without guidance on how to interpret and apply it. As one board chair in my research shared, "I think it is not sufficient to have reams of paper shoved at you. I think having a formal orientation where you walk through those expectations, I had to ask for that. It wasn't really brought to me, it was just expected that I would somehow know it." In the age of COVID, with social distancing and the prioritization of online communication, information-sharing for new chairs has become even more difficult.

If the role is this challenging, who are the insane few who *do* volunteer? And why do they do it?

Because there are zero financial incentives (in fact, board chairs are often expected to be lead financial donors, as well), the board chair position usually attracts two types of people who are motivated in different ways. The first type is drawn to the role out of altruism. These people really believe in the mission and vision of the organization and raise their hands because they know somebody must take the position. They're just stepping up to fill a need. Altruistic volunteers don't often take the role because they feel particularly prepared or believe they're the best person for the job; they do it because they want to make a difference.

The second type is more extrinsically motivated, often because they see personal potential in it. They take the position because they like to be in charge or believe the role could benefit them in some way (i.e., opportunities to network, learn new skills, or gain leadership experience). Whether someone steps into the board chair position out of altruistic desires or more extrinsic motivations, what they typically have in common is a lack of preparation. Even those who *think* they're prepared, usually aren't.

These challenges could be overcome with effective chair onboarding, but most nonprofits lack an onboarding system to make the process simple and effective. Small- to medium-sized nonprofits are typically resource-poor. They just don't have big operating budgets that cover costs like leadership training and investment in governance. Further, time is the most valuable resource for everyone in the sector. For this reason, it is important that executive directors have an onboarding process for new board chairs – one that can be easily tweaked and implemented each time a new chair takes the reins. Guidance for

EASILY developing an onboarding blueprint for any nonprofit is at the heart of this book.

If you're still not convinced about the importance of chair onboarding, consider this. A poorly onboarded chair is more likely to be an ineffective chair. A board chair can negatively impact the operationalization of a nonprofit's mission and vision within the community. Some of the challenges associated with an ineffective chair include:

- Leadership challenges resulting in a lack of direction and guidance for the organization
- Poor communication, misunderstandings, and conflicts
- Ineffective relationship with the executive director, which leads to burnout
- Negative and/or hostile board culture
- Decreased staff and volunteer morale

All these challenges can undermine the nonprofit's mission within the community. It is in the best interest of the nonprofit (and executive directors, in particular) to ensure a new board chair starts off on the right foot. A small but intentional investment at the start of a relationship with a nonprofit board chair, one that treats this role as a "new" position for a nonprofit volunteer, can save huge headaches down the road!

CHAPTER 3

Who is this Woman and Why Should I Listen to Her?

My entire career has been spent in the nonprofit sector, although, that wasn't really my plan from the start. After finishing my undergraduate degree in sociology and being accepted to a clinical psychology program, I deferred acceptance and spent time working for a nonprofit that offered experiential wilderness education for troubled teens. For a whole year, I worked with these adjudicated youth, living with them in the woods with no electricity in no-frills tents we constructed ourselves. Let me tell you, *that was an intense year.* I wager I can still light a fire in the rain, but I digress. While that time in my life was challenging and beautiful in many ways, it also opened my eyes (and heart) to the power of nonprofit organizations; what they give to us, what we can give to them, and the changes they can make happen. To me, nonprofit organizations are the glue that holds our society together and a powerful force for good in the world, no matter the focus, no matter the cause.

From there, I went on to spend 25 years working in nonprofit organizations as an internal leader and agent for change. In 2016, I founded my company, Centric Nonprofit Consulting, to help nonprofits achieve their strategic goals and solve common problems like— you guessed it—board chair onboarding and governance coaching. From the time I took my very first office job as a glorified fundraising envelope-stuffer, to my current role as executive director of a venerable 90-year-old west coast nonprofit focused on environmental protection (while often still stuffing envelopes) I have also served on nonprofit boards. And that's the unique perspective I bring to this work. Not only have I created/managed/led/implemented just about every aspect of nonprofit administration (one client once called me a "nonprofit Swiss army knife"), but I've also spent 25 years on the governance side of the table. I understand what an executive director needs from their governing board, as well as what a board needs from the administrative team.

When I decided to pursue my Doctorate in Organizational Change and Leadership at the University of Southern California, I knew I wanted to study the onboarding dynamics of nonprofit board chairs. In fact, my acceptance to this doctoral program was contingent upon me outlining a problem of practice I wanted to study and explaining why it was so important! I have observed *many* problems faced by nonprofits over the years, from the small and ordinary to the huge and extraordinary. Perhaps it's because of my job as Mom to two younger kids, but I feel every problem has a root cause that might just take a little digging to get to.

One enduring problem expressed throughout the sector, which I have personally experienced with dozens of nonprofits, is the tension between nonprofit boards and the internal administrative staff. Peeling back the layers to expose the root of the problem experienced by so many nonprofits revealed the ways an individual approaches the board chair role can significantly impact an entire organization. I wondered why nobody seemed to pay enough attention to board chair onboarding (or lack thereof) as a possible cause of many endemic institutional problems. I also wanted to know how high-performing board chairs navigated their new positions when they hadn't received the proper training to be a governing leader. The goal of my doctoral research was to shine a light on something that I believed, if addressed, could significantly improve operations and reduce the repeat pain-points of nonprofits, regardless of the organization's mission, focus, or budget size. So, before we start looking at the onboarding solution and how you can develop an onboarding blueprint for your own nonprofit, let's take a quick look at what my research revealed.

CHAPTER 4

The Research

The problem with the lack of chair onboarding is a persistent issue I've witnessed throughout my 25-year nonprofit career. When I began my doctoral program, my initial bias was that the problems were typically caused by the board chair; but my doctoral work and examination of my own biases as a researcher forced me to realize that this was actually a shared problem (with a viable solution). It had become evident (time and time again!) that many organizations expected chairs to learn the responsibilities of the role by observing during board meetings or drawing from their previous volunteer experiences. But what happened when a new chair came in without much experience with the organization? What happened if an incoming chair observed the dysfunction of a struggling board and thought that was the norm? And even if a new board chair was someone who had volunteered with the nonprofit for years, the roles of volunteers and board chairs don't routinely overlap. Without a structured way to learn the information needed to take the helm, chair succession is a bumpy ride full of frustrations for the chair, the executive director, other board members, and volunteers. The lack of chair onboarding creates problems that can trickle down throughout entire organizations.

I wanted to know how successful board chairs navigated their roles in the absence of onboarding. What were these people doing to overcome the hurdles and frustrations of chairing a nonprofit? Were they still frustrated and confused, but had some extraordinary coping skills? Were they lucky enough to have stellar relationships with their executive directors or an open line of communication with the previous chair? Perhaps they were retired and had copious amounts of spare time to dedicate to researching and learning everything they needed, on their own. By exploring the experiences of board chairs, I hoped to reveal the inadequacies of the onboarding processes used in small-to medium-sized nonprofits and come up with some recommendations for how to improve chair onboarding in these resource-scarce organizations.

Knowledge, Motivation, and the Organization

I'm flexing my creative muscles here to try to distill my 184-page dissertation down into a short and interesting summary. My query had three parts:

1. I wanted to understand the knowledge board chairs needed to possess to effectively fulfill their roles.
2. I wanted to know how a chair could be motivated to embrace and fulfill their roles.
3. Finally, I wanted to know what processes and procedures within a nonprofit either helped or undermined a new chair's abilities to fulfill the responsibilities of their role.

The foundation for my study drew upon Clark and Estes's gap analysis framework, which is based on the three tenets of knowledge, motivation, and organization (KMO).[1] Essentially, Clark and Estes argued that to reach goals, three things must be considered:

---

1   Clark, W., and Estes, F. (2008). *Turning research into results: A guide to selecting the right performance solutions.* Information Age Publishing.

1. The knowledge and skills possessed by people working on the goal;
2. The motivation of those workers to achieve said goal; and
3. Any organizational barriers to the goal that workers may encounter.

These tenets all interact to influence the outcomes of a project. For example, if your workers possess the required knowledge and skills and have all the organizational resources needed to reach those goals, *but* they all hate their jobs and think the project is stupid – well, they won't be very motivated to act. A project could still be completed without motivated workers, but it would happen much faster with inspired and passionate workers. Taking board chairs as an example, let's say an incumbent is highly motivated. They love the organization, believe strongly in its mission, and are ready to roll up their sleeves and get started in their new position. BUT, they only previously served as volunteers outside of the board work and lack the knowledge needed to be effective in the role. In that case, motivation is kind of like having 20 gallons of gasoline for a planned road trip, but no car to put it in.

Maybe someone takes on the board chair role and is both motivated and in possession of the knowledge needed to perform the role, BUT the organization is a disaster, board members hate each other, and the executive director is so overloaded that she's ready to have a nervous breakdown (been there, done that). In that case, organizational issues can create insurmountable barriers for a new chair.

Are you with me so far? For an organization to achieve its goals, the key stakeholders must possess the necessary knowledge, be adequately motivated, and work within an organization that doesn't create serious roadblocks. Let's take this a bit further and really examine each of these tenets.

Knowledge.

The starting point for assessing gaps in an organization is investigating what stakeholders know about an organization and its goals. This kind of assessment can also help align stakeholders to make sure everyone is on the same page. If key players possess different ideas of an organization's mission and objectives, projects will almost inevitably flounder. The tenet of knowledge can be further divided to include factual, conceptual, procedural, and metacognitive factors.[2] *Factual knowledge* includes the facts and details required to accomplish a goal. *Conceptual knowledge* describes an individual's familiarity with the domain they're operating within. *Procedural* knowledge refers to whether the stakeholder understands the necessary steps to attain their goal. Finally, *metacognitive knowledge* is having the self-awareness to recognize when more information or help is needed to achieve a goal.[3] The factors I focused on most in my study were factual, conceptual, and metacognitive.

Motivation.

Motivation is the catalyst that causes someone to take action toward a goal. It's what compels an individual to volunteer for the board chair position (or any role within a nonprofit). In the for-profit world, the main motivating factor is typically cash. Sure, someone may love their organization and co-workers, but the key factor that inspires them to get up every morning and dedicate a third of their waking hours to their job isn't a cool boss or neat projects; it's the compensation they receive for doing their job. In this way, for-profit organizations possess a key motivating factor that nonprofits do not. If a for-profit wants to attract top talent or increase worker output, it can offer financial incentives, which are typically pretty effective. This type of dangling carrot isn't available to the nonprofit sector. The absence of monetary motivators means nonprofits must tap into a deeper, more intrinsic motivation that can compel people to not only give freely of their time, but to invest themselves in the success of an organization.

---

2   Krathwohl, D.R. (2002). *A revision of Bloom's taxonomy: An overview. Theory into Practice*, 41(4), 212-218.

3   Krathwohl, *A revision of Bloom's taxonomy*; Rueda, R. (2011). *The 3 dimensions of improving student performance: Finding the right solutions to the right problems.* Teachers College Press.

Clark and Estes explained that motivation can be broken down further into *active choice, persistence,* and *mental effort.*[4] Active choice describes the decision to work on a task regardless of its desirability When people engage in active choice, they act based on their commitment rather than their feelings about a task. Active choice is sort of like Nike's famous motto, *just do it.* This tenet of motivation is especially important for board chairs, as the role often requires them to take on tasks that may feel beneath them (like stuffing envelopes or cold-calling prospective donors). *Persistence* describes a person's ability to stay focused on the goals at hand and continue working until objectives are met. Persistence is the willingness to dig in for the long haul, even when circumstances aren't ideal. Finally, mental effort is the level of effort required to engage in active choice and persistence. Mental effort can be undermined if a person is overly confident in their abilities, as they can then underestimate the work required to complete tasks. If someone views a task as beneath them, they may invest less mental effort, which can then impact active choice and persistence.

When these three motivational factors (active choice, persistence, and mental effort) are combined, performance and outcomes can improve.[5] A board chair may strive to see the value in the roles and responsibilities required of them without letting overconfidence cloud their understanding. Given the lack of volunteers for the board chair role, active choice and the desire to effectively govern (despite a lack of desire for the position), may help breed perseverance among those successful in the role.

Organization.

The final tenet of the KMO model is *organization.* While a number of factors can influence organizational outcomes, the most important organizational consideration within the nonprofit sector is culture. We can think of organizational culture as the product of joint learning experiences that create shared

---

4   Clark and Estes, *Turning research into results*
5   Clark and Estes, *Turning research into results*

assumptions about how to act and engage with one another.[6] Culture involves human interactions – ways of teaching people how to do new things, how to invest effort into those tasks, and the behaviors that are essential to achieving goals. Crappy organizational culture can derail even the most well-laid plans. The two cultural aspects of an organization that are most important when considering board chair onboarding and engagement are cultural model and cultural setting.

Cultural model is basically a group's shared understanding of how something works. There's nothing to see or touch, no relic or symbolic marker, just the lived experiences of your board members. Cultural model includes the attitudes and beliefs that influence how an organization operates, guiding group behaviors and creating pathways for learning and teaching among group members in a sort of cyclical way. As culture influences a board member's development, their behavior then creates the culture.

Cultural setting, on the other hand, is the idea that an organization's culture is influenced by the environment. More specifically, cultural setting is the organizational knowledge and language used to process it...complete with the biases and assumptions board members might bring (even if they don't mean to!). Words matter, particularly in the nonprofit sector, where each word of your mission statement grounds the work you do. I know these two concepts are a bit confusing, but they will come in handy when we get past this boring stuff and start thinking of them as tools to improve your governance culture.

Design

I used a mixed-method approach, which allowed me to gather multiple forms of data and triangulate my findings. Participants were selected from small- and

---

6   Schein, E.H. (2010). *Organizational culture and leadership (Vol. 2)*. John Wiley & Sons.

medium-sized nonprofits across the U.S. My parameter for organizational size was an annual operating budget between $500,000 and $15,000,000. I focused on nonprofits of this size because research indicates boards at this budget tier are often the most pressed for resources and have little in the way of investing in their boards of directors.

The first part of the study was an online survey that was completed by 32 current board chairs of nonprofits located throughout the United States. The survey consisted of 12 Likert-scaled items, three write-in demographic questions, and one open-ended question. I asked four closed-ended questions for each of the three KMO components. The second part of the study involved semistructured interviews, which were conducted with 23 of the individuals who completed the survey. I asked questions to better understand participants' experiences with the KMO components, probing for information on their behaviors, emotions, and opinions. Finally, I performed a document review to better understand aspects of each participant's organization, such as financial documents and statements about DE&I efforts.

The findings were eye-opening, confirming many of my suspicions and highlighting common challenges that board chairs experience when they assume the role, but more on that later. On average, survey respondents had served on their current board for 6.7 years; of that time, 2.3 years had been as board chair. Given that 88% of nonprofits set term limits, with most restricting membership to two consecutive 3-year terms with executive committee membership terms, and a more restricted 2-year limit on average, the survey sample provided a pretty accurate representation of the population.[7]

In line with nationwide research on board chairs, which indicated 83% of board members had no professional experience in the sector, 78% of my participants had no previous nonprofit volunteer experience, either. This statistic is incredibly important because it drives home the fact that most people who

---

7   BoardSource. (2021). *Leading with intent: 2021 national index of nonprofit board practices.*

hold the most powerful positions in nonprofit organizations have *no experience in the sector*! Like, none! While some experience in other sectors may apply, nonprofit organizations are a totally unique animal that requires specified training and knowledge to understand, much less, to lead.

Results

Knowledge

Okay, here's where it gets good, I promise. My first research question focused on the knowledge required by nonprofit board chairs to fulfill their responsibilities. I asked a series of questions to assess the three types of knowledge (factual, conceptual, and metacognitive). All 20 participants said they needed more specific knowledge about their organizations, as well as more global knowledge of the board chair's role and governing responsibilities. The participants provided a number of suggestions for ways to improve the transmission of specific organizational knowledge. Some of these strategies included:

- A handbook that detailed the organization's background and best practices
- Information on the history of the organization
- Access to current and historical governance documents
- Information about the organization's financial and nonfinancial metrics
- Information on the organizational culture, think SWOT analysis

While it can be difficult for board chairs to access specific organizational knowledge on their own, participants in my study took a lot of personal initiative to access general knowledge about how nonprofits operated and what the role of board chair entailed. Global information sought by the participating board chairs included things like setting meeting agendas and learning how chairs should be involved in strategic planning. Some quotes from the participant interviews that best illustrated these proactive behaviors included:

- "I'm looking for opportunities to learn what it means to be a board president. So, any resources that I can access, I'm accessing."
- "When I found out I would have to be board chair, I went ahead and read everything I could get my hands on."

The internet was a heavily cited source for accessing global knowledge, with participants taking to Google to learn what they could on their own. These findings indicated that board chairs – at least those participating in my study – were generally motivated people accustomed to autonomy and taking the lead. While it's great that they took the initiative to learn what they could on their own, an onboarding system could streamline this process and reduce the likelihood of disconnects in expectations regarding basic aspects of governance. For example, if a new board chair comes across advice that contradicts the practices and systems already in place within an organization, unnecessary frustrations with the executive director and other board members may arise. Plus, if a new board chair doesn't have to use their limited volunteer time to go out and search for information about what the heck they're supposed to do in their new role, they can dive right into actual governance work in support of your nonprofit!

Regarding conceptual knowledge, one-quarter of my participants didn't feel extremely comfortable discussing their organization's mission and vision. While none of the participants said they felt uncomfortable discussing these things, I was a little taken aback that 25% were only "somewhat comfortable" with the core components of the nonprofits they led. During the interviews, participants' lack of familiarity with their organization's mission and vision became even more concerning. Seventy percent of the interview participants admitted that after they became board chair, they realized that didn't understand the organization's mission and vision as well as they thought. Eighty percent of the interview participants said their understanding of their organization's mission increased substantially *after* becoming the leader. A properly onboarded chair would possess the conceptual knowledge they needed to perform their roles at the onset of the position, not *after* they assumed the most powerful leadership position in the organization.

Some interesting findings also emerged regarding participants' metacognitive knowledge. Not only must a board chair possess the factual and conceptual knowledge to effectively perform their role, but they must also be able to identify where their personal knowledge gaps exist and then take action to fill those gaps. That is, board chairs must be able to recognize *what they don't know*. To address knowledge gaps, half of the interview board chairs discussed receiving mentorship from the previous chair. These participants described ongoing meetings and open lines of communication with previous chairs, which were fundamental in helping them learn everything they needed to know about their responsibilities. Document analysis indicated that for organizations with past board chairs that provided connection and mentorship to their successor, 70% named previous board chairs on their public rosters. This simple act could create an unspoken norm that encourages previous chairs to make themselves available to the new chairs and serve a helpful role in onboarding.

In terms of their relationships with executive directors, most participants felt they worked well together. A board chair's reflexive awareness of their own leadership style could be key to productive relationships between executive directors and board chairs. Many of the chairs interviewed in this study described metacognitive adaptations that fostered healthy relationships with their executive directors. For the most part, they wanted to serve as a resource to help the director, not to "take over" or micromanage. These participants were reflective of the ways they could grow and improve their own understanding of their governing role while recognizing factors that could impede their abilities to perform their duties.

Many participants described problems with a lack of time, both in terms of their own time but also as a matter of accommodating the needs and schedules of busy board members. Many participants described a willingness to bring on consultants to help fill in the gaps in their knowledge about nonprofits, as well as the humility to accept help and training from others. The participants possessed an awareness of their knowledge gaps and then took steps to address them. Outside of seeking the advice of consultants and mentors, they talked a lot about learning through observing. When transitions were planned, they were able to carefully observe the behaviors of current chairs to learn how to fulfill the duties when they took over. However, transitions were often abrupt or unexpected, so learning through observation wasn't always an option.

Participants also learned by leveraging input from staff members. For example, one interview participant said, "It's helped me tremendously that I live close to the nonprofit and I could interact with the leadership and full-time staff." Another participant said they gained specific knowledge of their organization through their connection with staff, elaborating that,

"I've become very good friends with the team, we have 30 full-time staff and I probably know all of them." The lucky few who had previously served as board chairs for other organizations were able to leverage their broader understanding of board chair governance gained from those previous roles, which was sometimes helpful. Others utilized community resources, such as affinity organizations and online groups, to connect with peers and learn about the board chair role.

Motivation

A nonprofit board chair may possess all the knowledge needed to govern an organization, but if they lack motivation, they will not be very effective.[8] Participants in my study seemed to be very intrinsically motivated – which is probably the case for most volunteer positions. Excitement about the mission

---

8   Clark and Estes, *Turning research into results*; Rueda, *The 3 dimensions of improving student performance*

of the nonprofit and the desire to use their personal or professional skills were the primary motivators for 16 of the interview participants. Many participants had been personally touched by the organization and viewed volunteering to serve on the board as a way to "give back."

Other participants were motivated by the perceived value that chairing could provide them with, both professionally and personally. One-quarter of participants admitted to becoming involved with their organizations to strengthen their professional ties and gain social capital. One participant joined the board of their organization just 7 days after moving to their new company, on the advice of their supervisor to get involved in the community. Another interviewee shared, "My client was actually the executive director of the nonprofit…and she suggested that I join."

The ability to apply their experiences and skills to help the organization was another motivating factor for participants. While only one interview participant had prior professional experience within the sector, many interviewees expressed a reliance on their past professional experiences to inform their preparation for nonprofit governance. Participants were also motivated to make improvements to various aspects of their organizations, such as governance. All board chairs were motivated to use their skills to improve the onboarding process for future board leaders and/or improve aspects of the governance framework. Their personal experience of transitioning to the board chair role and lack of onboarding support spurred them to improve the process for their successors. Self-efficacy, while not directly tied to motivation, may have also been a motivating factor for participants. The more capable and confident they felt in their abilities to perform their duties as chair, the more motivated they were to assume the role of board chair.

Organization

Results from my study indicated that organizational procedures and processes impacted the board chair's ability to effectively fulfill their governance responsibilities.

The two ways organizations impacted chairs' governing abilities were through the cultural model and cultural setting. The organizational culture within which the board chair operates is a constructed understanding of how the nonprofit works; it is a model formed from underlying assumptions that guide the influences and behaviors of all organizational members.[9] The lack of resources was an aspect of organizational culture that was detrimental to participants. Interview respondents mostly felt that their organizations provided them with few materials to help with their onboarding. Two of the three board chairs who stated they were partially onboarded shared their lackluster experiences: "Throwing booklets or attachments at someone and saying, 'here's your orientation, go for it' is not conducive to really bringing someone in, in a positive way and building them up or equipping them for their new role." Another interviewee expressed that although they worked closely with the outgoing chair, "nobody gave me instructions."

In addition to a lack of resources, a lack of organizational procedures created organizational impediments for participants. When their role within the governance framework was unclear, board chairs struggled to prevent their discord from reaching fellow volunteers. One board chair shared, "I was honestly quite frustrated and not feeling like the board was something I wanted to be a part of at all." Other organizational issues cited by respondents included the internal turnover of top managers and communication breakdowns between board chairs, members, and executive directors. Many board chairs interviewed cited a focus on rebuilding these internal relationships to strengthen their organizations with a focus on procedures related to communication and connection. Chairs were acutely aware of the importance of cooperative relationships with executive directors. While half of the respondents described relationships with their executive directors as strong, others admitted these relationships were strained or fractured.

---

9   Gallimore, R., & Goldenberg, C. (2001). *Analyzing cultural models and settings to connect minority achievement and school improvement research*. Educational Psychologist, 31(1), 45-56.; Rueda, *The 3 dimensions of improving student performance*

Foundational to strong internal relationships within the organizations was communication. All 20 board chairs interviewed said they frequently met their executive directors, with most respondents meeting on a weekly basis. Regular interactions with executive directors helped board chairs feel supported by their organizations. The use of language and the development of trust were also emphasized as important communication components by participants.

Using the Findings

My research underscored how necessary it is for board chairs to possess specific knowledge about their organizations. Results highlighted the intrinsic motivators that often drive board chairs, especially their passion for the nonprofit's mission and the desire to apply their skills effectively. Self-efficacy also emerged as a significant motivator, as confidence in their abilities increased motivation to fulfill their roles effectively. Findings further revealed the impact of organizational procedures and culture on board chairs' abilities to fulfill their responsibilities. Issues such as lack of resources, unclear roles, and communication breakdowns hindered effective governance. Strong relationships with executive directors and clear communication were identified as crucial for successful board chairing. By providing onboarding that addresses knowledge gaps, fosters intrinsic motivation, and cultivates a supportive organizational culture, executive directors can empower board chairs to navigate their roles with confidence, contributing to the success and sustainability of the organizations they serve.

Okay, you made it through the academic stuff – sorry about all that! Now let's put it all together to create an onboarding solution that you can develop and implement at your organization.

PART 2:

The Solution

CHAPTER 5

Inform and Educate

If you made it through the exciting chapter on my research (no judgment if you passed it over), you know I organized my study by the knowledge, motivation, and organization (KMO) model. I wanted to understand the knowledge board chairs needed to fulfill their roles, how a chair could be motivated to embrace their new duties, and what organizational processes could influence their ability to serve as needed. My results revealed that new board chairs required two types of knowledge: specific factual knowledge, and more general, global knowledge. Let's take a look at *what* each type of knowledge entails.

Specific Factual Knowledge

Specific factual knowledge includes the facts and details required to accomplish a goal within the organization, whether that involves setting a meeting agenda, developing a budget, or creating new programs. Board chairs must understand what their organization stands for, its values, its operation, and its history. Before we dive into the details you should share with your new chair, I want to share a quick note about the importance of transparency.

No matter how difficult it may be to assume complete transparency about the specific facts of your organization, it is absolutely imperative that you tell incoming chairs the *whole truth*. One of the biggest frustrations expressed by board chairs in my study was that they didn't really know what they were getting themselves into when they volunteered for the role. One of my participants lamented that they had been "sold a false bill of goods," which they accepted without really understanding the scope of the board chair's burdens. The transition into the board chair role often revealed discrepancies between expectations and reality among the board chairs in my study. One participant admitted feeling misled during the recruitment process, stating, "Once I started as board chair I understood the organization better but not in a good way…like peeling layers of an onion." Additionally, inadequate understanding among board members about the organization's functions further compounded the challenge. "I mean, it was amazing the number of people I've talked to on the board that really didn't understand the basic function of what we do," remarked one participant.

Here's the thing: none of my participants indicated they wouldn't have volunteered if they *had* been privy to the hornet's nest they were walking into when they took on the role. Even if they had been aware of the secret mess in the organization, their passions and motivations would have still led them to volunteer. The difference is, they would have felt more prepared for the role they were stepping into.

As tempting as it may be, try not to sell prospective board chairs a rainbows-and-unicorns fantasy about your organization. Be upfront about any internal or external challenges the organization is up against and be open to solutions your new chair may have, as well as the amount of time they can anticipate putting into the role. The failure to be transparent may not only lead to frustrations for your new chair and board members, but could also cause sudden turnover, internal strife, and splintered relationships among your key stakeholders. Always, always, *always* strive to be honest about what the board chair position entails, an estimate of the time commitment required to be a productive governing leader, and any current challenges you're facing. It's a great idea to include a write-up of the position's governing responsibilities and any current issues within your organization to share with your new chair (more on that at the end of this chapter).

Details about the organization's background, mission, and vision

Some of the most critical information needed by a new chair is what makes up the heart and soul of your organization: its background, mission, and vision. Nonprofits are organized around these fundamental elements, and you'd be surprised how many folks accept board chair positions with murky understandings of these key items. A whopping 70% of my study participants admitted they didn't understand their organization's mission as well as they thought when they accepted the board chair role. Seventy percent! And these participants were arguably a cut above the rest, as highly effective and motivated individuals who had already put in their time as volunteers and board members with their organizations! While some participants felt they gained a deeper insight into the mission as board chairs, others found themselves peeling back layers of complexity. "As board chair, I do feel like I understand the organization better...for better or worse," remarked one participant.

With that said, it's important to make sure your board chair understands your organization's mission, vision, and history. When and how was your organization established? What are your guiding principles, including the mission and vision statements? In what ways does your organization help individuals or communities? This orienting information is a great place to include some inspiring stories of people whose lives have been changed through the organization. The goal of this information is to make sure the new chair understands what the organization stands for and excite them about contributing to the organization's mission. Words matter and your mission statement allows you to connect emotionally with your new chair, sometimes word by word. Remind them why they were motivated to serve on your board, and why they raised their hand to take on a governance leadership role. Help them understand how valued and appreciated they are because, after all, a nonprofit can't exist without a board chair (for real, legally it can't!).

Access to current and historical governance documents, including financial statements

In addition to understanding the heart of your organization, the board chair must have access to current and historical governance documents, as well as current financial information. Key financial information the board chair may benefit from includes profit/loss statements, 990s, balance sheets, and annual reports from the previous 2-5 years. It's also possible your chair may need some help understanding nonprofit financials, so be conscious of that and show a willingness to meet with them to go through the information together. Financial literacy emerged as a significant challenge for many new board chairs. One participant admitted, "It was tough to learn about our finances... an area I needed to work really hard at." Another highlighted the nuances of nonprofit finance, stating, "It's still counting beans, it's still finance, but you have different rules and regulations at a nonprofit."

The lack of comprehensive information about the organization's operations left new chairs feeling unprepared, but many were proactive once they realized where their own knowledge gaps existed. Always encourage your chair to ask questions. Never assume they know what's going on just because they were in board meetings. Research shows that many board members don't speak up in group settings to better understand nonprofit financials, and the lack of nonprofit financial comprehension is a root cause of role ambiguity. Although in my own organization I have a highly experienced board chair who I respect immensely, you better believe I'm sitting down with them to go over financials because you never know! I've outlined some examples below of governance documentation information you might include.

A discussion of the non-financial metrics used in your organization

Because most board chairs lack nonprofit experience, they're often accustomed to measuring success solely in terms of financial metrics. It can be challenging for them to wrap their heads around nonfinancial metrics as success measures, so it's important to provide information on what these things are and how they're measured in your organization. Most likely, these all exist in some form or fashion for your grant and funding applications, but your board chair might not be familiar with them. Some of the key nonfinancial metrics commonly used in the nonprofit sector include:

SOCIAL IMPACT INDICATORS: These indicators quantify the outcomes and changes brought about by your organization's activities. They may include measures such as lives impacted, beneficiaries served, communities reached, or even qualitative indicators of changes in people's behaviors, attitudes, or well-being.

PROGRAM EFFECTIVENESS: Nonprofits assess the effectiveness of their programs through metrics related to program outcomes, outputs, and efficiency. Indicators of program effectiveness could involve things like program completion rates, quality of services provided, client satisfaction, or the number of individuals or communities served through the organization's programs.

VOLUNTEER ENGAGEMENT: As you know, nonprofit organizations usually rely on volunteers to carry out their missions, so volunteer engagement is an important factor to measure. Metrics related to volunteer engagement may include the number of volunteer hours served, rates of volunteer retention, volunteer satisfaction, or the quality of volunteers (such as skill diversity and commitment).

STAKEHOLDER ENGAGEMENT: The engagement of key stakeholders in a nonprofit is also a valuable non-financial metric. Engagement might be indicated by things like stakeholder satisfaction, interactions with the broader community, or the quality of partnerships formed with other organizations. Some of the measures of stakeholder engagement might include donor retention, feedback from beneficiaries, or partner satisfaction surveys.

ADVOCACY AND AWARENESS: If your organization focuses on advocacy or raising awareness about specific issues, you might assess things like the social impact of your campaigns, influences on policy or public perception, media mentions, or increases in your organization's social media following.

ORGANIZATIONAL CAPACITY: Nonprofits often assess their capacity and effectiveness through metrics related to organizational health, governance, and sustainability. These measures could include things like staff turnover, staff satisfaction, fundraising efficiency ratios, or the organization's adaptability to changing circumstances.

Information on the organization's financial metrics

While board chairs with professional backgrounds in the for-profit sector will be familiar with the use of financial metrics, these are still different from those used in the nonprofit sector. Your board chair may know all about increasing the bottom line through improvements in worker efficiency, products, or services, but do they know how to fundraise? Are they familiar with the donor process? Just like any organization, yours requires income to thrive, but board chairs without sector experience may be stumped by how financial targets are set and achieved in the nonprofit sector. The information you share about financial metrics should go beyond the operating budget and expenses to also focus on how money is generated in your organization. Here are some of the key financial metrics commonly used in the nonprofit sector:

REVENUE STREAMS: Nonprofits must keep track of revenue sources to pinpoint where their funding comes from. These sources may include donations, grants, program fees, and membership dues. Understanding different revenue streams can help nonprofits diversify their funding sources so they aren't reliant on any single source.

FUNDRAISING EFFICIENCY: The efficiency of fundraising efforts is another important financial metric to track, as this allows organizations to gauge the effectiveness of different strategies. Fundraising efficiency is calculated by comparing the cost of fundraising activities to the funds raised through those efforts. Common ratios for fundraising efficiency include the fundraising expense ratio (which is the total fundraising expenses divided by the total contributions) and the cost to raise a dollar (which is fundraising expenses divided by total contributions).

PROGRAM EFFICIENCY: Program efficiency is also essential to understand, as this metric reveals how efficiently organizations use resources to deliver programs and services. Program efficiency may be calculated by comparing total program expenses to outputs or outcomes. Common calculations for program efficiency include the cost per beneficiary served, cost per service delivered, or cost per outcome achieved.

OPERATING RESERVE RATIO: Your organization's ability to weather financial storms and cover short-term expenses is the operating reserve ratio. This metric is a comparison of net assets to annual expenses. A solid operating reserve ratio is an indication of the organization's overall financial stability.

OVERHEAD RATIO: Finally, overhead ratio is a comparison of administrative and fundraising expenses to the organization's total expenses. Overhead costs are normal and necessary for organizational operations; however, a high overhead ratio could indicate inefficient management of funds. This metric can vary significantly across nonprofits, depending on the complexity of different programs and services offered, so be sure your targeted overhead ratio is aligned with your organization's needs.

Information on the organizational culture

Organizational culture is a hot topic in the for-profit world because business leaders understand how valuable culture is within any organization. Likewise, organizational culture plays a pivotal role within the nonprofit sector, shaping its operations, effectiveness, and impact. At its core, organizational culture represents the collective values, beliefs, behaviors, and norms that guide interactions and decision-making within an organization. It serves as the foundation upon which impactful work is built, driving cohesion, innovation, and resilience in pursuit of social change. In the nonprofit world, where missions often revolve around social causes and community betterment rather than profit, cultivating a strong and positive culture is important – and often overlooked.

Think of it this way – a vibrant organizational culture helps create a sense of purpose and unity among staff, volunteers, and board members. Nonprofits rely heavily on the dedication and passion of their members, and a strong culture reinforces their commitment to the organization's mission. When people feel connected by a shared purpose, they're more likely to be motivated and engaged contributors.

Organizational culture can also have a big impact on a nonprofit's ability to fulfill its mission. A culture that prioritizes transparency, creativity, collaboration, and innovation can enhance problem-solving, decision-making, and adaptability. Positive organizational culture encourages open communication that allows stakeholders to communicate concerns and ideas while working collaboratively toward common goals. I will talk more in-depth about the importance of organizational culture and how to create it in Chapter 9, but I wanted to categorize it here as specific factual knowledge your new chair should be presented with during onboarding.

Descriptions of the roles and responsibilities of board members, staff members, and volunteers

Board chairs should know who's on the organization's team as well as their roles and responsibilities. When you make sure new board chairs understand the key roles of different stakeholder groups (i.e., staff, volunteers, and other board members), you can help them govern more effectively. A clear delineation of the duties of these different groups within the organization can help the board chair make sure everyone involved contributes to the mission. Also, as executive director, this can help the new chair clearly understand differences in the responsibilities of executive directors and chairs, and help prevent anyone from stepping on someone else's toes, right from the start.

When your board chair understands the roles and responsibilities of everyone in the organization, they may be able to communicate their expectations more clearly. This clarity helps prevent misunderstandings, conflicts, or inefficiencies that may arise from ambiguous or overlapping roles. Understanding the capabilities and contributions of key stakeholders can also help the chair delegate more effectively to achieve organizational goals. When the board chair understands the roles and responsibilities of each group, they can facilitate collaboration and mutual support. This creates a cohesive organizational culture and maximizes the organization's overall impact.

A calendar of events

Help your board chair stay abreast of key events held by your organization by sharing a calendar of events that will take place during their time of service. Be sure to update the calendar as needed to reflect the most current events and describe their role at these events. There is an expectation of attendance, a board chair is a public-facing role after all, but taking it one step past that will only help acclimate your new chair for improved effectiveness. One of my research participants was even handed talking points to guide their public comments for each event they had to participate in! In 25 years of working in this space, I had never heard of that, but it can brilliantly decrease the burdens and anxiety your board chair may experience in their new role.

Global Knowledge

Okay, now that we've discussed the key elements of the specific factual knowledge a new board chair should have access to, let's talk about the more global knowledge they may be lacking. Over the years, I've noticed that many new board chairs come into the role without some of the basic skills needed to be effective. It's just assumed that because they served on the board before, have business leadership experience, or have volunteered with the organization, they'll know how to take the lead as chair. I've also noticed that new chairs often feel uncomfortable asking questions or worry they may be viewed as incompetent if they admit to not knowing *exactly* what to do as chair. As executive director, you can help your new chair circumvent this sense of inadequacy by sharing the global knowledge they may need. The three key pieces of global knowledge that new chairs often benefit from include information on how to lead meetings, how to communicate across the board, and how to handle conflict.

HOW TO LEAD A MEETING. A key responsibility of nonprofit board chairs is leading board meetings. They play a critical role in setting meeting agendas, leading meetings, and ensuring time spent in board meetings is productive and aligned with the organization's objectives. Here are some strategies you can share with your new board chair to help them successfully lead meetings.

Set clear objectives. Setting clear objectives and agendas is essential. With your assistance, board chairs should communicate meeting goals in advance and develop an agenda that outlines topics for discussion, timeframes, and desired outcomes.

Stay on track. It can be easy for a meeting to get sidelined if a chair doesn't know how to keep the board on track. Maintaining focus and staying on track during board meetings is important – people have carved out time to attend the meeting and that time should be respected. Board chairs should guide discussions, make sure the time is managed well, and redirect any off-topic conversations.

Encourage participation. Your chair should lead meetings where people feel encouraged to participate. By promoting active participation among board members, your chair can foster engagement and collaboration, which can have positive effects that trickle down throughout the organization. All board members should feel free to share their perspectives, ideas, and insights during meetings.

Create a respectful culture. While this tip is really part of the overall organizational culture that should be fostered in your organization, board chairs need to ensure meeting settings are always respectful. Derogatory comments and insults should never be tolerated. Your board chair should make sure all voices are heard in meetings, and that all viewpoints (diverse as they may be) are considered.

Be a decision-maker. Board chairs should be comfortable with making decisions. They should be able to guide discussions toward a group consensus and make sure decisions ultimately align with the mission and objectives of the organization.

Seek feedback. Lastly, chairs should seek feedback from board members (and you) to help them evaluate their meeting effectiveness. Feedback can help them continuously improve their skills and outcomes.

HOW TO COMMUNICATE ACROSS THE BOARD. The second area of global knowledge that board chairs can often use some help with pertains to communication across the board. Communication skills are vital for an effective nonprofit board chair; just because someone served on the board or has outside leadership experience doesn't automatically mean they're expert communicators or know how your nonprofit manages the channels of communication within your organization. You can help your chair foster transparency and collaboration among board members, and ensure everyone's work is grounded in your mission by making them aware of a few of these key strategies:

Establish clear communication protocols and channels. Board chairs should schedule regular board meetings, send email updates, and use other internal communication systems that you may have access to, like BOARDnetWORK.org, to keep board members informed about organizational activities, challenges, and opportunities.

Keep an open door. As previously mentioned, board members should have the opportunity to feel heard and recognized; board chairs can foster this by having an open-door policy. This can encourage board members to voice their opinions, concerns, and ideas freely, even outside board meetings.

Active listening. Not only should the board chair engage in active listening, but it should be a set expectation among all board members during meetings. Active listening helps foster understanding, empathy, and respect across the board. Help your chair understand that they are facilitators of board discussions.

HOW TO HANDLE CONFLICT. Finally, conflict management is a required skill for anyone in leadership positions, but many leaders struggle to deal with conflict. Shirking from conflict or responding in an inflammatory manner can just worsen organizational rifts. As the top leaders of nonprofits, board chairs must know how to manage conflict within the organization because – and I hate to say it— conflict at the board level can easily infiltrate the entire organization and have repercussions in areas from board recruitment to fundraising. Yikes!

Conflict management skills help chairs to effectively navigate disagreements and maintain harmonious governance. Conflicts within the organization should be handled constructively, through healthy dialogue and problem-solving and always stressing to your board chair that their colleagues are volunteers. I've always found that puts things into perspective, stressing that no one in that board room HAS to be there…they WANT to be there.

Effective conflict resolution can preserve relationships, promote consensus-building, and prevent serious disruptions to organizational goals. By honing conflict management skills, board chairs cultivate a culture of respect, trust, and accountability. The key conflict management skills of effective board chairs include active listening and communication, as previously discussed. In addition, board chairs can employ empathy, mediation, problem-solving, emotional intelligence, and proactive prevention strategies to deal with internal conflicts.

EMPATHY. Understanding the emotions and motivations underlying conflicts can help board chairs address root causes and find mutually beneficial solutions. Empathy fosters trust and builds stronger relationships within the board. Board chairs should be encouraged to put themselves in others' shoes when conflicts arise, to help understand all sides of a disagreement.

MEDIATION. During conflict within the board, chairs should take on a mediator role to facilitate negotiations that help identify common ground among oppositional viewpoints. Board chairs should try their best to remain neutral and objective.

PROBLEM-SOLVING. Effective conflict resolution requires analytical thinking and problem-solving skills. When conflict arises, board chairs should identify the underlying issues and consider various solutions to address them.

EMOTIONAL INTELLIGENCE. Although emotional intelligence is often considered a personality trait, research indicates it can be learned and developed. Board chairs with high emotional intelligence are often better at managing their own emotions and those of others during conflicts. An emotionally intelligent chair can stay calm and diplomatic, even when conflicts become heated.

DECISION-MAKING. When mediation and communication fail to reach a mutually satisfactory outcome, board chairs need to be able to step up and make decisions on behalf of the organization. There will be times when conflict within the board requires decisive action. Board chairs should be able to make tough decisions, when necessary, ultimately focusing on the best interests of the organization and its stakeholders.

CONFLICT PREVENTION. Arguably, the best way to deal with conflict is to prevent it from occurring in the first place; this can be done by creating an organizational culture that facilitates respect, transparency, and collaboration (more on this in Chapter 8). Through healthy organizational culture and communication, board chairs can proactively address potential conflicts before they escalate.

Packaging the Information

Alright, now you know the different pieces of information your new board chair may benefit from (and hopefully an inkling of why onboarding of this role is so important!). But how do you package all the information up for them with the smallest amount of effort on either of your parts? Again, I know how busy you are (been there) and I also know how limited your board chair's time is (done that). Well, that's up to you, but you'll want to make sure it's as organized and transferable as possible. Once you put the initial effort into gathering and organizing this information to help onboard a new board chair, subsequent onboarding will require far less effort and become a part of your governance culture specific for your board chair. The two ways I recommend packaging the information is either through a three-ring binder or a backpack. If you're going for extra credit, you can place the binder in a backpack (joking, kind of), along with some thoughtful freebies, like a notepad, a couple of pens, stickers, magnets, or whatever other marketing materials you already have on hand. Personally, I like the backpack idea because it creates a literal object that can be passed from the former board chair to the new one, during the symbolic changing of the guard. By adding a thank you card, you can show your chair that not only do you appreciate their willingness to volunteer for the role, but also that you want them to feel prepared and supported as they assume their new responsibilities. Maybe it's just me, but I love writing thank you notes, hence why they are mentioned a few times in this book!

A key thing to remember is that board chairs must be provided with essential information in practical, bite-sized pieces. Chairs are volunteers who have lives outside of the organizations they work with, so it's essential to provide them with information in an efficient manner. This is why an onboarding binder or backpack is so great and again, over time, it makes your work much easier and strengthens your governance framework.

It's also important that new chairs don't feel like their executive director has just shoved reams of paper at them once they take over. As great as the on-boarding backpack or binder is, you should also take some time to go through the information with your new chair. You don't need to read through everything together, line-by-line, but make it a part of your bi-monthly/monthly meetings to go through the information so your new chair has an opportunity to ask questions. One of my study participants noted their frustration when they were provided with some documentation but told nobody would review it with them: "The outgoing chair sent over materials a couple days in advance of my taking over and then told me in an email that there was no time to review them!"

Dedicating this up-front time to meeting with your new chair can go a long way in setting the tone for an amicable, productive relationship between the two of you, which is worth its weight in gold. Bonus points? Do it outside of the office! Research shows time and time again that social connection builds trust and accord, so grab a cup of coffee or a glass of wine and chat about the role.

Alright! Now you know all the different types of knowledge your new chair needs during onboarding. It's time to chat a bit about how to motivate them to be the stellar performers you need them to be.

CHAPTER 6

Motivate

Now that you know *what* information your new board chair should be provided with during onboarding, let's discuss how to motivate and inspire them to be awesome, effective leaders. As executive director of a nonprofit, you know all about the strange dynamic between board chairs and executive directors. You may have been with your organization for years, molding it from your own blood, sweat, and tears. Then, every year or two, you're tasked with recruiting and probably training a new board chair, who's essentially your boss....even though they might not understand the role (or heck, even want it!). That odd dynamic places you in an awkward position when it comes to motivating your board chair. You don't technically have the authority to tell them what to do (which usually doesn't go over too well), but you need them to be motivated to collaborate with you for the benefit of the nonprofit you're both leading. This is where understanding how to leverage intrinsic and extrinsic motivation can be of value as you onboard your new chair.

Intrinsic Motivation.

Intrinsic motivation is a fundamental concept in psychology that focuses on an individual's innate drive to engage in an activity for its own sake rather than for an outside reward. Intrinsic motivation can derive from personal satisfaction, a sense of fulfillment, or enjoyment received from working on a task. Unlike extrinsic motivation, which involves outside factors like tangible benefits, intrinsic motivation is internal and associated with an individual's values and interests.

At its core, intrinsic motivation is driven by internal factors such as curiosity, passion, and a desire for personal growth and mastery. People who are intrinsically motivated are more likely to persist when challenges arise and experience a deep sense of fulfillment from their efforts. Intrinsic motivation is the lifeblood of nonprofits because tangible rewards, such as salaries and bonuses, aren't available to the volunteers who contribute so much. Intrinsic motivation is usually what inspires your volunteers to roll up their sleeves and board members to voluntarily show up for meetings. A nonprofit volunteer who is intrinsically motivated may derive immense joy and meaning from contributing to a cause they care deeply about, even without compensation or recognition for their efforts.

In the workplace, intrinsically motivated employees are more productive and committed to their work, leading to improved organizational performance and morale. Understanding intrinsic motivation is essential for leaders in nonprofit organizations as they seek to inspire and empower volunteers and staff to achieve the organization's goals. By fostering a culture that nurtures intrinsic motivation, nonprofit leaders can cultivate a sense of purpose, autonomy, and passion among all stakeholders, ultimately driving greater impact and creating sustainable success. Not only is it important for you to inspire intrinsic motivation in your board chair, but you also want your board chair to foster intrinsic motivation among the rest of the board.

The psychology of intrinsic motivation
The psychology of intrinsic motivation delves into the underlying mechanisms that drive individuals to engage in activities for their own inherent satisfaction

and fulfillment. Intrinsic motivation is influenced by factors like autonomy, mastery, and purpose. Autonomy refers to the sense of control and self-direction individuals experience when they have the freedom to choose their actions and pursue activities aligned with their interests and values. Mastery involves the intrinsic desire to improve skills and achieve personal growth and competence. Purpose relates to the deeper meaning and significance individuals find in their pursuits, often helping them feel connected to something bigger than themselves. By tapping into these psychological drivers, leaders can create environments that nurture intrinsic motivation, leading to greater engagement, productivity, and well-being.

The role of intrinsic motivation in nonprofit leadership

Imagine walking into a bustling nonprofit organization dedicated to providing education and resources to underprivileged communities. You're greeted by a team of enthusiastic volunteers and staff members, each driven by a shared sense of purpose and commitment to the organization's mission. What fuels their passion and dedication? You already probably know the answer – intrinsic motivation.

At the heart of every nonprofit is a noble mission - whether it's fighting hunger, promoting education, or protecting the environment. This mission serves as a beacon, attracting individuals who resonate deeply with its goals and objectives. For these individuals, contributing to the nonprofit's mission isn't just a job or a task; it's a calling, a deeply ingrained desire to make a positive impact on the world.

Moreover, nonprofit organizations are built on a foundation of core values, like integrity, compassion, and social justice. These values guide every aspect of the organization's work, shaping its culture, decision-making processes, and interactions with stakeholders. Individuals who are intrinsically motivated are drawn to nonprofits whose values mirror their own, creating a harmonious alignment that fuels their commitment and dedication. Intrinsic motivation and the mission and values of nonprofit organizations are intertwined. This connection fosters a vibrant organizational culture, fuels innovation and creativity, and ultimately, empowers nonprofits to create lasting positive change in the world.

Unique motivating factors in the nonprofit sector

Within the nonprofit sector, intrinsic motivating factors drive individuals to volunteer their time to advance organizational missions. A number of distinct intrinsic motivators power the nonprofit sector, including the following:

MISSION ALIGNMENT: One of the most powerful intrinsic motivators in nonprofits is the alignment between an individual and an organization's mission and values. People are drawn to nonprofits whose missions resonate with their personal beliefs and passions. The opportunity to contribute to causes they care about on a profound level serves as a powerful driver of engagement and commitment. Organizations must elect chairs who align strongly with the nonprofit's purpose, as they will be more inherently motivated than individuals who volunteer for the board chair role to achieve status or some other outside benefit.

IMPACT AND MEANINGFULNESS: Nonprofit work provides people with the chance to make a difference in the world. Many volunteers and staff members are intrinsically driven by the satisfaction they get from knowing their efforts are meaningful. Whether they're driving social change or reducing suffering in some way, the sense of impact and meaningfulness are strong intrinsic drivers. When board chairs feel like their efforts are impactful, they are more likely to thrive in the role. You can promote meaningfulness by alerting your chair to the ways they are driving positive change through your organization.

SENSE OF COMMUNITY AND BELONGING: Many people volunteer with nonprofits because of the sense of belonging their involvement creates. People like to feel camaraderie and the experience of shared commitment within a supportive and welcoming setting is a strong intrinsic motivator. A positive organizational culture will foster this sense of belonging. You can leverage this intrinsic driver with your new board chair by ensuring they feel welcomed and integrated into the organization. For your chair to lead effectively, they should feel like they are the head of the organizational family, and the culture of belonging and community will then trickle down throughout the organization.

PERSONAL GROWTH AND DEVELOPMENT: Even though nonprofits rarely have the resources to provide training and professional development, they offer a fantastic setting for people to grow and develop new skills, experientially. People who volunteer with nonprofits may be intrinsically motivated by opportunities for personal growth and learning through their experiences. Nonprofits provide fertile ground for individuals to expand their knowledge, hone their talents, and acquire new skills while contributing to meaningful causes. The intrinsic satisfaction derived from continuous learning and self-improvement further fuels engagement and commitment within the nonprofit sector. If you know your new chair raised their hand because they wanted opportunities to grow and learn, be sure they have those experiences while they're at the helm. During your initial conversations, ask your chair if there are any specific growth experiences they hope to have during their tenure, and then offer suggestions for ways to actualize those hopes.

Why intrinsic motivation should also be fostered among board members, staff, and volunteers

Every executive director dreams of leading a nonprofit driven by board members, staff, and volunteers who are genuinely passionate and committed to the organizational mission. Intrinsic motivation is the secret sauce behind individuals' unwavering dedication. You don't only want a board chair who is intrinsically motivated, but you want a leader who can foster intrinsic drive among everyone involved. In the realm of nonprofit organizations, fostering intrinsic motivation among board members, staff, and volunteers isn't just a nice-to-have; it's a game-changer.

First, intrinsic motivation ignites passion and purpose. When individuals are driven by their internal desires and values, they bring a high level of enthusiasm and dedication to their roles. Intrinsic motivation also fosters greater engagement and retention among volunteers. Intrinsically motivated individuals are more likely to be actively involved and go above and beyond their responsibilities. This high level of engagement increases volunteer and staff retention, which contributes to the long-term stability of an organization. Finally, intrinsic motivation drives creativity and innovation. Individuals who are internally motivated are more inclined to think outside the box, take risks, and explore new approaches to addressing social issues. This spirit of innovation is essential for nonprofits to adapt to changing circumstances and maximize their impact within the community.

Strategies to cultivate intrinsic motivation

As executive director, there are two main ways you can cultivate intrinsic motivation, not only in your board chair, but among all stakeholders in the organization. First, you can establish a purpose-driven organizational culture. In nonprofit organizations, it's not just about what we do, but *why* we do it. When your organization is infused with a sense of purpose, you can ignite a fire within your team members that fuels their passion and commitment to the cause. Be sure to clarify your organization's mission and values. What are you here to achieve, and what principles guide your work? Communicate these foundational elements clearly and consistently, to ensure everyone, from the board chair to the volunteers, understands and aligns with the organization's mission.

You can also lead by example, embodying the values and principles you want to instill in your board chair. Demonstrate passion, integrity, and dedication to the organization's mission in everything you do. Your authenticity will inspire others in your organization, from the top down, to do the same. You can also foster intrinsic motivation within your chair by empowering their autonomy. Make sure they feel free to take ownership of their work and contribute their unique talents to the organization.

Also, be sure to recognize and celebrate your chair's wins. Acknowledge the impact of their efforts, big or small, and celebrate milestones with them along the way. Simple acknowledgment can help reinforce your chair's sense of purpose and motivate them to continue making a difference. Highlighting your chair's achievements not only boosts their morale but also inspires others to follow suit. Recognition is more valuable when it's personalized, so take the time to express gratitude directly, acknowledging your chair's specific contributions and their positive impact. Personalized recognition shows that their efforts are seen, valued, and appreciated.

Address burnout

Before I go much further, I want to make a quick note about burnout because it's very common in nonprofits. I'm willing to bet *you've* probably grappled with at least a touch of burnout over the course of your nonprofit career. Burnout feels like hitting a wall because you've become so emotionally, mentally, and physically depleted from stress or overwork. Unaddressed, burnout can leave its victims feeling drained and disillusioned, to the point where even the smallest tasks feel insurmountable. Because burnout can cause people to check out, leader burnout is particularly dangerous to organizations. Here are a few quick tips for addressing burnout, both among yourself and your board chair.

First, prioritize self-care. It might sound cliché, but taking care of yourself is crucial when you're in the business of caring for others. Make sure you're getting enough rest, eating well, and exercising regularly. Set boundaries around your work hours and make time for activities that recharge you, whether it's spending time with loved ones, pursuing hobbies, or simply taking a break. I know, easier said than done, but I had to put it in print.

Next, build a support network. Surround yourself with colleagues, friends, and mentors who understand the unique challenges of nonprofit work and can provide encouragement, advice, and a listening ear when you need it. Don't be afraid to reach out for help or seek professional support if you're struggling – and make sure you communicate this to your chair, as well. It can also be helpful to create opportunities for peer support and debriefing sessions that can not only signal support to your chair but also strengthen the relationship between the two of you.

Finally, at the risk of sounding like a broken record, don't forget to revisit your organization's mission and values, regularly. Reconnect with the purpose behind your work and remind yourself of the positive impact you're making in the world. Keeping your sense of purpose front and center can help you stay motivated and resilient to burnout. If you start to detect burnout in your board chair, have a conversation in a caring and compassionate manner. If they're feeling overburdened, help them delegate responsibilities to others within the organization.

Ok, I know that you, like me, probably won't take much of this guidance. I actually found it hard to address burnout and take my own advice during my own time in the hot seat, even though I'd spent years coaching executive directors and board chairs! While the above suggestions are evidence-based, here's a gem that I've picked up from lived experience that I wanted to include here. I've served for many years on the board of a local community services nonprofit, led by an executive director who I deeply admire. She is one of the most effective leaders I've ever encountered, and I don't say that lightly. When I was in a governing leadership role with her, she had a fantastic phrase that would humanize any discussion and had the power to shift the tone of a conversation; "If I can be vulnerable with you right now." As the listener, you can't help but slow down and listen more actively and with more empathy. As the speaker, I have found it allows me to share with my own governing leaders, a problem I might have kept to myself or something that I'm really struggling with that might paint me in a less-than-invincible light. Just keep it in mind – I've never experienced a bad result from its genuine usage.

Extrinsic Factors

While the strongest motivational factors in nonprofits are undoubtedly intrinsic in nature, I would be remiss to ignore a few powerful extrinsic motivators. Extrinsic motivators are those that come from outside sources, like money, praise, or even avoiding punishment. In the for-profit world, people may be extrinsically motivated in two ways: (a) to earn pay/advancement opportunities/bonuses, and (b) to avoid getting fired. In the nonprofit world, where most workers are uncompensated volunteers, extrinsic motivators look different, but they still exist. For nonprofits, extrinsic motivation usually takes the form of prestige, impact, and networking opportunities. In fact, some of my own research participants were very honest that their reasons for joining their nonprofit board were extrinsic in nature (such as securing new clients or seeing their name on the masthead of the organization).

Recognition and prestige

Executive directors can publicly acknowledge the contributions and achievements of board chairs at board meetings, staff gatherings, or organizational events. By highlighting their successes in front of their peers and stakeholders, you can reinforce their value and importance to the organization. Taking the time to provide personalized praise and recognition to board chairs can have a powerful impact. You can send your chair handwritten notes, emails, or messages expressing gratitude for their hard work, dedication, and leadership. I don't want that to seem like a burden or an extra note to be added to your already steep pile, but personalized appreciation shows board chairs that their efforts are seen and appreciated on an individual level.

You can also celebrate milestones and achievements reached by your board chair during their tenure. Whether it's reaching fundraising goals or achieving strategic objectives, acknowledging these accomplishments reinforces the board chair's sense of accomplishment and encourages continued dedication and effort. Even an honor for the term of service, a gift certificate purchased through your budget or small contributions from their board colleagues, goes a long way not only in celebrating your chair, but helps those who might be considering the role know that your nonprofit appreciates the work!

Influence and impact

By involving board chairs in decision-making processes and seeking their input on key initiatives, you can make them feel like valued contributors to your organization's success. This sense of influence can be a powerful motivator, inspiring board chairs to take ownership of their roles and make a meaningful impact. Board chairs like to know their efforts are making a difference – that they're not just spinning their wheels, but actually driving positive change within the organization and the community they serve. You can highlight what your chair's goals are and their progress towards them throughout their tenure, showing board chairs (and again, future board chairs watching from the sidelines!) the tangible results of their work can be incredibly motivating.

Board chairs may also be extrinsically motivated by opportunities to use their skills in a nonprofit leadership setting. An overwhelming majority of

respondents cited their experience in leading teams as a primary professional skill they brought to the table. This demonstrated a commitment to leveraging their expertise to drive positive change within the organization. Many
board chairs were not shy about advocating for their organization's mission
and values using their communication skills. As one participant stated, "I'm
not shy about giving voice, both in writing and in speech, talking about what
is, for me, the important ethical grounding of [nonprofit] in our community."

Networking opportunities

A final extrinsic motivator for board chairs relates to opportunities to network.
Most board chairs want to feel connected – to other leaders, influencers, and
experts in their field. For some participants in my study, motivation extended
beyond a desire to give back or feel purposeful; they were inspired by networking and community involvement opportunities. As one participant shared, "I
had done a little bit of [volunteer] work in my former location and found it a
great way, selfishly, to network and become part of the community." This desire
to connect with others and be an active participant in community initiatives
served as a driving force for many.

By providing networking opportunities, you can help board chairs expand
their professional networks, build relationships, and tap into new opportunities for collaboration and growth. One way to do this is by inviting your
chair to accompany staff at networking events, outreach opportunities, or local
fundraisers where board chairs can connect with other nonprofit leaders, community partners, and potential donors. These events not only provide valuable
opportunities for your nonprofit in regard to building your community pres-
ence, but also expose board chairs to new ideas and perspectives within the
nonprofit sector. Your board chair might also derive fulfillment and be motivated to serve through donor and funder meetings. Having been on both sides
of the equation as an internal member and board leader, your chair might be
thrilled to be included in a fundraising ask with you (or they might run for the

hills… but as my mom used to say, it's always nice to be asked!). And let me tell you, having them participate can be incredibly impactful. It demonstrates that your nonprofit values your board, that they are active participants in your strategies, and that your board chair values your mission enough to volunteer on an ask. It's a win-win for building meaningful connections, organizational knowledge sharing, and helping motivate your entire board.

Small side note, and I hope this goes without saying, but your chair (or any board member for that matter) should never go out on their own to meet with funders and make solicitations on behalf of your organization without you knowing about it and being present. I actually brought in a mediator many years ago for a conflict between an executive director and board chair, when the board chair went off solo and had a meeting with a very major donor that staff had been working with. It was a real challenge and a lesson in what not to do!

CHAPTER 7

Communicate and Collaborate – In Brief

Along with the importance of informing and motivating a new board chair, the onboarding process should emphasize the development of a healthy, effective relationship between you, the executive director, and your board chair. By far, one of the biggest challenges that executive directors face with new board chairs centers around communication and relational difficulties. Board chair turnover often places executive directors in the uncomfortable position of training someone new on the responsibilities of their role (which include being their boss). It's often a weird dynamic for both parties and a reason why most groups overlook chair onboarding; but awkwardness aside, this is the governing structure of all nonprofits.

You can often dramatically improve the interpersonal experience with your new board chair by putting in some upfront effort to foster a communicative and collaborative partnership. The executive director-board chair relationship is the most influential dynamic in nonprofits; not only will your relationship-building efforts improve your professional experience (by having a symbiotic rather than antagonistic relationship with the chair), but these benefits will trickle down throughout the organization.

How can you foster fabulous collaboration and partnership with your new board chair? The simplest and most effective strategy is to have regular meetings with them. Create opportunities to discuss challenges and concerns, and make sure you're both on the same page regarding programs, the use of resources, the direction of the organization, and any interpersonal issues that may be happening. Schedule meetings at regular intervals (these may be weekly at first, and then extend out to monthly meetings after the chair is fully onboarded) and set a clear agenda for each meeting. Participants in my study spoke at length about the value of regular communication with their executive directors. As one shared, "We have a weekly zoom catchup where we just talk about what's on our plates and what we think we need to address…we established that right at the beginning when I came in as board chair." Another explained that they kept in frequent contact with their director and "the lines of communication are always open."

Check in with your board chair regularly to see how things are going, address any concerns or challenges, and make sure you're seeing things eye-to-eye. Planning for a small amount of time on your packed schedule to foster a cohesive relationship with your chair will help create a trusting dynamic so when problems do arise, you both will be better equipped to deal with them.

Establishing Clear Expectations

Sit down with your board chair and have an open conversation about roles, responsibilities, and goals. Be transparent about what you expect from them and what they can expect from you. This sets the stage for a productive and collaborative relationship from the start.

During this meeting, outline the key areas where you'll need their support and involvement – whether through fundraising, strategic planning, or community outreach. Be clear about the time commitments, communication channels, and decision-making processes involved so there's no confusion down the line.

Build Trust and Rapport

Building trust and rapport with board chairs is key to fostering a collaborative partnership that drives the mission forward. Take the time to get to know your board chair on a personal level. Grab coffee, have lunch, or even just chat before or after board meetings. Building these informal connections helps create a foundation of trust and understanding that's essential for collaboration.

Be transparent by regularly sharing information, updates, and challenges with your board chair. Let them know that you value their input and perspective. And always follow through on your commitments; if you say you're going to do something, do it! Demonstrating reliability and accountability builds trust and confidence in your leadership. Additionally, be open to feedback and constructive criticism. Welcome input from your board chairs and be willing to listen, learn, and adapt (personally this is a real challenge for me, we are the paid "experts" at running the nonprofits after all!). I have worked with nonprofit leaders who ignored everything their chairs suggested to them, simply because they viewed them as not experienced enough in the sector to have viable ideas. I know it's hard to cultivate an openness to suggestions, particularly in this dynamic when the line in the sand between administration and governance *should* be so clear, but you never know when your chair's perspective might be an amazing one! Executive directors can get stuck in their silos, and board chairs are there to help crack a window now and then. Demonstrate integrity, honesty, and professionalism in your interactions with your chair and within the organization as a whole. When you model these values, it sets the tone for a positive and collaborative partnership.

Provide Support and Guidance

Supporting and guiding board chairs is crucial for fostering a collaborative partnership that propels the organization forward. Be available to coach your chair. Again, I know how full your plate is, but try and take time to provide guidance and feedback to your board chairs. Whether it's helping them navigate complex issues or develop leadership skills, your support can make a world of difference to them as well as the governance culture you are building.

Be sure your new chair has access to the resources and information they need, especially those items covered in Chapter 5. When necessary, be a sounding board for your chair. Encourage open dialogue and create a safe space for them to share their thoughts and concerns. When concerns do come up, address them constructively and proactively. Don't sweep issues under the rug – tackle them head-on with honesty and a focus on finding solutions. In doing so, you'll foster a relationship of respect. As one of the board chairs in my research admitted, "We have disagreements, but we have them in such ways that like, we're thoughtful about the words we're saying and the potential impact they have on others." By handling conflicts positively and collaboratively, you demonstrate your commitment to the partnership and the organization's mission. And it's worth mentioning again, your next board chair is most likely watching from the wings!

We've tackled the knowledge and motivation facets of the KMO model, in terms of chair onboarding. It's time to move on to the organizational factors you should keep in mind when bringing on a new chair. Let's begin with organizational culture...

CHAPTER 8

Create Culture

Strong organizational culture is essential to the success of nonprofit organizations. However, like chair onboarding, the importance of organizational culture is often overlooked. Resource constraints, such as limited time and limited funds, may lead to the prioritization of programs and service delivery over culture-building (the actual delivery of your mission!). Such constraints can ultimately cause board chairs and executive directors to focus on external relationships with stakeholders who provide financial support, rather than the internal organizational dynamics. Failure to understand the impact of organizational culture can also hinder efforts to build it and stymie your nonprofit's mission and impact.

While nonprofits may struggle when it comes to creating and delivering organizational culture, for-profits often spend significant money on internal culture. Consider some of the leading organizations in the U.S., known for their dynamic and effective organizational culture. The internal cultures of these companies mirror and drive organizational values. Take Google, for example, a technology powerhouse known for its innovative workplace culture that encourages the pursuit of creative ideas, collaboration, and risk-taking. Or Southwest Airlines, celebrated for its employee-centric culture that prioritizes teamwork, servant leadership, and a fun-loving atmosphere. Patagonia is a personal favorite of mine – an outdoor gear company known for its commitment to environmental sustainability, social responsibility, and employee well-being. Patagonia's organizational culture reflects its values of environmental steward-ship and activism, offering employees opportunities for outdoor adventures, environmental initiatives, and work-life balance.

For-profit organizations invest in company culture because they under-stand how strongly culture influences success on every level. Mega-businesses have lots of money to throw organizational culture initiatives – a luxury that bootstrapped nonprofits typically lack. But, culture is just as important (dare-say, even *more* important) for the nonprofit sector. While nonprofits lack the ability to incentivize stakeholders with salaries and bonuses, culture can play an important role in intrinsic motivation for volunteers, staff, and board mem-bers. And I hate to mention but funders and the public at large? Yep, they'll know if your culture is off!

Defining Organizational Values and Beliefs

The first step in creating a kickass organizational culture is to define the val-ues and beliefs of the organization. Think of this as going a step beyond your organization's mission and vision. While the mission and vision represent the *what*, organizational culture colors *how* your organization operates. What's it's pulse? How do volunteers connect with the organization? What keeps employees coming to work each day, and what's the inspiration that drives your board members to continue giving freely of their time?

Organizational culture, often likened to the vibe or atmosphere of a work-place, is the collective values, beliefs, behaviors, and norms that shape the identity and character of an organization. It's the intangible essence that permeates every aspect of an organization, influencing how people interact, make decisions, and work toward common goals. Think of it as the underlying rhythm that sets the tone for daily operations and interactions—it's the way things are done "around here." Yet, despite its pervasive influence, organizational culture often remains an overlooked tool in driving organizational success. This oversight is a missed opportunity, as a strong and positive culture can foster employee engagement, creativity, and innovation, while also attracting and retaining top talent.

At the heart of this culture are the core values and beliefs that shape the organization's identity and guide its actions. Identifying and articulating these values is the foundational step in creating a cohesive and purpose-driven environment. These values serve as the organization's moral compass, guiding decision-making and behaviors at all levels. Make sure your organization's mission and vision are woven into all the activities and communication that take place.

Beyond core values, shared beliefs and principles further define the organization's culture. These beliefs represent the collective mindset of the organization and shape its interactions, both internally and externally. Articulating shared beliefs can foster unity and coherence among team members, reinforcing a sense of purpose and identity. Share impact stories of how the organization has affected real people in the community, especially at board meetings. These stories can provide opportunities for the board to see the value and impact of the organization in practice, which can foster a sense of culture and commitment. I had one of my research participants call this exercise an "essence story" which I loved, and they shared it was essential for emphasizing and reminding everyone of WHY they were in the boardroom.

Values and beliefs play a central role in shaping organizational culture and influencing how members interact and collaborate. By aligning values with actions and decisions, nonprofits can cultivate a positive and supportive culture that empowers individuals and drives collective success. Moreover, a strong organizational culture built on shared values enhances employee engagement and fosters innovation in the face of challenges. Involve the board chair in creating a shared organizational culture. When everyone is bound together by a shared commitment to a nonprofit's mission, they are better prepared to overcome obstacles and disagreements be they small or large!

Leading by Example

As the leader of the organization, the executive director can shape the culture of a nonprofit through their actions and attitudes. By consistently demonstrating the values and principles that define the organization, the executive director sets the tone for others to follow. Whether it's fostering collaboration, promoting transparency, or embracing diversity, the executive director's actions speak volumes and influence the culture of the organization.

Authentic leadership is also key to building trust and credibility within the organization. The executive director must demonstrate authenticity, integrity, and accountability in their interactions with staff, board members, and volunteers. Transparency and honesty can inspire confidence and foster a culture of openness and trust. The executive director's leadership actions should inspire staff, board members, and volunteers to embrace the organization's mission and contribute meaningfully to its success. By fostering a culture of empowerment, the executive director enables individuals to take ownership of their roles and make valuable contributions towards shared goals.

Fostering Open Communication

The culture within a nonprofit is heavily influenced by the nature and effectiveness of communication within the organization. Executive directors can lay the foundation for effective communication through transparent information-sharing. Establishing clear channels for communication ensures information flows freely and transparently throughout the organization. Whether through regular staff meetings, email updates, or an intranet platform, providing avenues for sharing important information keeps everyone informed and engaged in the organization's activities and decision-making processes.

In addition, encouraging open dialogue fosters a culture of inclusivity and innovation. By creating opportunities for all stakeholders to voice their opinions and share ideas, you can promote a sense of ownership and commitment to the organization's mission and goals. Embracing diverse perspectives and fostering collaboration leads to better decision-making and problem-solving outcomes.

Effective communication practices are instrumental in building trust and rapport within the organization. By communicating openly, you demonstrate integrity and authenticity, which are foundational to building trust among stakeholders. Listen, show empathy, and be responsive to concerns and feedback you receive from others in your organization – especially from your board chair.

Promoting Collaboration and Teamwork

Because nonprofits require the collaborative efforts of many stakeholders, another important aspect of organizational culture involves teamwork. Executive directors can create opportunities for collaboration that foster innovation and synergy across the organization. A culture of teamwork also strengthens the organization's collective capacity and resilience while creating a sense of camaraderie and solidarity within the organization. Acknowledge and celebrate group achievements and successes to reinforce a culture of collaboration and teamwork. Whether through team recognitions, awards ceremonies, or informal celebrations where teams meet in person, you can demonstrate appreciation for the contribution of staff and volunteers, fostering a positive and supportive work environment.

Embracing Innovation and Adaptability

Strong organizational culture is also one that embraces innovation. I know this is a buzz word (often with expenses attached to it) that many reading this book may not think is not relevant to the nonprofit sector. It took me a long time as a leader in the field to realize that innovation doesn't mean risk-taking with stakeholder funds; it means thinking of new ways to serve your mission and embody your values. Encouraging creativity, fostering a culture of continuous learning, and embracing change are vital to cultivating an innovative and adaptive organizational culture within nonprofit settings. Executive directors can inspire creativity and innovation among staff and volunteers to cultivate a dynamic and forward-thinking organizational culture. Explore new ideas and develop innovative solutions to existing problems. Foster a supportive setting where failures are viewed as opportunities; by doing so, you can empower volunteers, staff members, and the board to unleash their creative potential.

Because the world is changing faster than ever, nonprofits must be able to embrace change and adapt to the evolving needs of individuals and communities they serve. Agility is essential to navigating the dynamic landscape of the nonprofit sector…ever have a major funder who gave one year, you planned on their contribution for the next based on all available information, and then nothing but a huge budget hole to fill your next fiscal when they stepped away? Adapting to evolving needs and challenges requires a willingness to embrace change, pivot strategies, and explore new opportunities. By fostering a forward-thinking culture of adaptability, you can position your organization to respond effectively to changes and seize new opportunities for growth and impact.

Assessing and Cultivating Culture

Finally, assess the culture of your organization and make changes as needed.

Actively solicit feedback from staff, board members, and volunteers to gain new insights into the organization's culture. By seeking input and creating channels for transparent communication, you demonstrate a commitment to the needs of the organization and its members. Hold regular feedback sessions, distribute surveys, and conduct focus groups to provide opportunities for individuals to share their experiences and ideas for improving the organizational culture.

A Note on Organizational Culture and Board Culture

As stewards of an organization's mission and values, the executive director and board chair play a pivotal role in shaping the culture and direction of the nonprofit. While nonprofit leaders can implement the suggestions I've offered to create a powerful, positive, and productive organizational culture, it's important to recognize the unique impact of the micro-culture within the board. Think of the board culture as the tip of the spear – the culture in the boardroom will inevitably trickle down throughout the entire organization. Remember this when creating culture, especially if the culture within your board needs some sprucing up. Help your board chair build a strong culture at the board level and notice how the whole organization is positively impacted. The culture at the top will inevitably influence the culture throughout your nonprofit, and all the recommendations I've provided in this chapter may be useful throughout the entire organization.

CHAPTER 9

Plan for Succession

A discussion on nonprofit chair onboarding would be incomplete without an emphasis on succession planning, a top pain point for nonprofit boards and internal leaders across the country. While the limits to board chair terms are a bummer, they also create a structure that executive directors can plan around. If you know that you'll have to bring in a new board chair every one to two years, you can start planning for that succession well in advance. Depending on what your bylaws say, you might even need to start the process at the very first meeting with your newly appointed slate (I know, I'm so very sorry for mentioning that!). Executive directors should work closely with their governance or nominating committee to consistently look at the pipeline of potential successors and be mindful of who will take the reins when a current chair's term limits have been reached.

Involve the current chair

From the start, nonprofit board chair succession planning must involve the current (and even former) board chairs. Not only can these individuals offer valuable insights that can help ensure future recruits are a strong fit for the role, but involving them in recruitment can also help set an expectation that will keep them involved throughout the entire succession and onboarding process, which we'll dive into in the next chapter. Involving current and former board chairs in recruiting successors is a strategic approach that leverages their insights and experiences. Give your new board chair a little time to get settled, and then it's never too early to have a conversation about the succession plan. Discuss their thoughts and preferences regarding the qualities and skills they believe are essential for their successor to possess now that they have held the seat themselves rather than observing what the role needs from around the boardroom table. This dialogue lays the foundation for collaboration and can help ensure alignment between the outgoing and incoming board chairs. Not only will this alignment foster continuity within the organization, but a former board chair will be more likely to stay involved throughout onboarding (and be more engaged in their own!) if they have had a role in recruiting the individual they are passing the baton to.

Leverage the knowledge and experience of current board chairs to inform the recruitment process. Seek their input on candidate evaluation criteria, interview questions, and selection criteria. Their insights can help ensure the recruitment process is thorough and aligned with the organization's needs and priorities. By involving current board chairs in recruiting their successors, you can tap into their expertise to identify candidates who are well-aligned with the nonprofit's goals and challenges, which few others understand as well as the current board chair.

There's one other important consideration during recruitment that probably goes without saying if you've held your role as executive director for any length of time, and it's this: when recruiting a new board chair, think about how well the two of you will work together. Depending on your organization, this might be the role of a committee who will hand you a slate of officers rather than include you in the process, but I strongly encourage you to make your voice heard! This isn't just about making sure you don't bring in a new chair that drives you nuts, but more so an acknowledgment of the trickle-down effects that the board chair-executive director relationship can have on an entire nonprofit. This dyadic relationship is the front line for your nonprofit, and the dynamic between these two leaders can significantly impact the organization's effectiveness and success. A harmonious relationship built on trust, respect, and effective communication fosters collaboration and alignment toward shared goals. Conversely, a poor fit between the executive director and board chair can lead to friction, power struggles, and inefficiencies that hinder progress and undermine the organization's mission.

Research has shown that strong leadership partnerships are associated with improved organizational performance, increased stakeholder satisfaction, and enhanced strategic decision-making. Therefore, executive directors must prioritize compatibility and synergy when recruiting new board chairs, ensuring that both professionals share a vision for the organization's future and possess complementary skills and perspectives. By fostering a positive and productive working relationship between the executive director and board chair, nonprofits can maximize their impact and effectively navigate the challenges of the ever-evolving nonprofit landscape. Remember that 75% of board chair-executive director partnerships end in conflict or departure from the nonprofit. Be the 25%, build your board leadership pipeline and let your voice be heard!

CHAPTER 10

Mentorship

The last essential key to effective board chair onboarding is mentorship. Mentors can provide invaluable guidance and support to new chairs who are learning to navigate their roles. Through mentorship, newly onboarded chairs can gain valuable insights and practical advice. Ensuring crossover with an outgoing board chair prevents a new chair from feeling like they've been thrown to the sharks, helping them make informed decisions and avoid common mistakes from the start. Of course, I'm about to map out an ideal situation because, as the research shows, many incoming board chairs are greeted by an empty seat to fill since the last board chair took off running, BUT you can prevent that all-too-common situation with some takeaways from this book!

Arguably, the most valuable mentor to a new chair is an individual who previously served as a successful chair for your nonprofit. Not only can a former board chair provide inside guidance and information on process and procedures specific to your organization (because remember, every nonprofit is different!), but their involvement in onboarding a new chair can foster continuity and stability that strengthens the governance culture. For participants in my study, learning from the experiences of former board chairs offered valuable insights. "Learning from a former board chair provided an opportunity on how not only to approach the role, but also how to interact with my executive director," remarked one of my research participants, emphasizing the importance of mentorship and knowledge transfer in facilitating a smooth transition into the board chair role.

By passing down knowledge and best practices from one generation of leaders to the next, mentorship ensures the organization's mission and values remain intact throughout leadership changes. Both the procedural knowledge of how to do the job and the knowledge of how a board chair fits within the culture of your nonprofit STAYS within your organization and becomes part of your nonprofit framework.

Mentorship also promotes collaboration and relationship-building, helping your new chair to build rapport and strengthen their networks within and around the organization. Former board chairs who serve as mentors can help connect new chairs with key stakeholders, connect them to important resources, and help them more effectively navigate boardroom dynamics.

Mentorship can provide your new chair with a trusted ally and guide as they step into their new role.

Encouraging previous board chairs to mentor their successors

So, how do you convince a former chair to volunteer *more* of their time to the organization after they've finished their duties? It's not nearly as difficult as you might think. The truth is that most people want to help, feel useful, and have opportunities to share their expertise and insights. Keep this in mind when reaching out to former board chairs and emphasize the unique insights and wisdom they can provide to incoming chairs based on their tenure and accomplishments. Make it clear that their guidance can make a meaningful difference in shaping the future direction of the organization. Remind former and outgoing board chairs of the lasting legacy they've left behind and how mentoring their successors can help ensure the organization's continued success and growth. Emphasize the opportunity to pass down their knowledge, values, and leadership insights to the next generation of leaders.

It may also help to provide incentives and recognition. Offer formal recognition or honors to former board chairs who participate in mentorship programs, acknowledging their ongoing contributions to the organization's mission and success. Place their names on the organization's masthead as Former Board Chair or Past Board President to build public accountability for their work. You can also consider creating networking or social events that bring together current and former board chairs, which can provide opportunities for informal mentorship and relationship-building. And if all else fails? Build the expectation of mentorship from outgoing to incoming as a part of the board chair role at your organization. Just knowing that there will be some guaranteed crossover will help a new board chair feel supported and more effective as a governing leader from day one.

CHAPTER 11

The Blueprint

Okay folks, we've made it to the final chapter. You've explored the challenges of board chair onboarding with me. We've waded through my research together. We've combed through the onboarding solution, highlighting the importance of knowledge, motivation, communication, culture, succession planning, and mentorship. Now, it's time to pull it all together into the onboarding blueprint. Where to begin? Well, let's pack those backpacks!

Onboarding backpack (or binder, or file, or whatever you choose)

Although no one wants tons of documents to read through, all the board chairs in my study were self-educated and sought out the information they needed to do their jobs. Think of how much more effective they would be if your organization provided all the information they needed in a simple, organized backpack, saving them time and frustration! Little effort, big reward. The key here is to provide the necessary information in a condensed and organized way, within some sort of package that can be easily transferred from one chair to the next (I have the image of an Olympic torch handover in my mind as I write this). There are samples of a universal board chair packet on my website at www.centricnonprofitconsulting.com for free. Use it, share it, and tailor it to the needs of your organization.

The nonprofit board chairs who gave their time and insight to participate my study sought learning opportunities independent of the organizations they served because they were motivated to succeed in the role. Additionally, all board chair participants shared they were working on aspects of the onboarding process that weren't present when they assumed the role and/or were striving to enhance the culture of their organizations in some way. Their learning about the board chair role was not an organic aspect of their board service: interview participants understood this significance and sought to bridge this learning gap for their successors. This was not a question within the interview protocol, yet all board chairs found the time to share a gap they experienced within the governance framework and cultural improvements they were striving towards. I say all this to drive home the value of providing an onboarding backpack. This is a great opportunity for you, as executive director, to simplify the onboarding process in an efficient and effective manner. A little upfront work that will pay off in a big way over the life of the organization and this information will *stay* with your nonprofit and become a self-maintaining part of the governance culture.

Were a board chair to begin their role onboarded, with mentoring, and feelings of support, their knowledge and motivation may be utilized more effectively to invest in goal attainment targeted to organization improvements and mission delivery. All interview participants in my study reinvested back into their governance framework: from improving onboarding for their successors to elevating the importance of mission with their peers to instituting shared learning opportunities. Their specific and global governance knowledge did not vanish upon their departure, it stayed within their nonprofits and strengthened them, thereby justifying investment in the board chair's onboarding. This was my big "light bulb" moment from my research!

Formalize the onboarding role of the previous board chair

Set the expectation for continued involvement of your predecessor chair, potentially even allowing for a period of term overlap. In my study, 100% of participants expressed a desire to enhance the onboarding process for their successors and ensure a seamless transition (because they themselves had not experienced it). And they planned on being there for the next board chair to fill their seat. Establishing a leadership pipeline becomes feasible when incoming chairs understand that their predecessors are willing to assist them in acclimating to their new role. Public recognition of the previous chair, such as listing their name on the masthead and formalizing the transfer of responsibilities and knowledge they accrued during their tenure, can foster greater accountability and accessibility of information for the incoming chair. This simple adjustment can counteract the perception of the board chair role as transient, infusing it with a sense of permanence and formalizing the imperative of knowledge transfer.

If your next board chair has previous volunteer experience at your nonprofit and the time to serve, lock them down!

You're seeking a committed partner for your organization's leadership. Interestingly, 80% of the individuals in my study had previously volunteered with their nonprofits before assuming the role of board chair. This pre-existing involvement fostered a deeper appreciation for the organization's mission and willingness to serve as a board leader. Many of them described how their volunteer experiences motivated them to rally fellow board members around a shared vision and values. They structured board meetings to highlight operational successes and actively engaged all members in shaping a unified understanding of the nonprofit's mission.

Leveraging active volunteers for future board leadership positions may offer a more enriching recruitment strategy. Having contributed to its achievements firsthand, these individuals are already deeply engaged, familiar with the organization's intricacies, and invested in its success. Despite identifying a candidate with the requisite skills and interest for the board chair role, organizations often overlook the significance of a volunteer's time commitment in achieving strategic goals. Roughly half of the interviewed board chairs in my study were professionally retired, with many others boasting flexible schedules that allowed for greater dedication to their roles. It's crucial to ensure that anyone assuming the board chair position has the necessary time to serve effectively. While someone might be highly motivated for the role, be sure to assess whether they have the time and availability to fulfill the commitment of serving as board chair.

Demystify the role

Be transparent, about the work, the finances, the culture, etc. Don't be scared! It's really not that bad! I know that feeling of desperately needing someone – *anyone* – to step up and fill the board chair position. But don't paint an inaccurate picture of the board chair duties just to get a warm body in the seat. Comprehensive national research, alongside findings from my study, indicate there's great hesitancy to take on the board chair role. The question is, why? Could it be the personal time required to successfully fulfill governance duties? Lack of clarity around roles and responsibilities and the importance therein? Insufficient understanding of the true state of the nonprofit they are asked to lead? Perhaps it's all three.

Within my study, 70% of interview participants didn't fully understand the operationalization of the mission prior to becoming board chair, while 80% reported they understood the mission better *after* becoming board chair.

I have personally been approached to take on the role of board chair, and only through lived experience was able to ask the questions necessary to discern the true state of the nonprofit, which was quite different from what was presented to me. I declined the role, not because of the challenges that awaited, but because of the lack of honesty in discussing all aspects of their operations.

Find out why your chair is serving, and feed their need!

Seventy-five percent of the participants in my study shared that they were drawn to the board role by a desire to leverage a specific skill or expertise. Because this trend extended to their decision to assume the board chair role, it's crucial to understand their underlying motivations. My research underscored the importance of conducting a thorough exploration of their intentions and aspirations. Many participants expressed that a simple SWOT analysis would have been beneficial in identifying where their strengths could be best utilized within the organization. Hence, it's imperative to engage in open dialogue with your new board chair to uncover their driving forces, what they hope to contribute, and their goals for their tenure. By aligning their motivations with the organization's mission and objectives, you can empower them to make a meaningful impact and foster a sense of fulfillment in their role.

Self Evaluations for the Win

Establishing an effective onboarding process for your board chair is not a one-time event but rather an ongoing journey. Just as you, as the executive director, seek to feel empowered in your role, your board chair desires the same sense of efficacy. Self-evaluation is a valuable tool to provide to your board chair and can catalyze meaningful discussions. However, the responsibility for evaluation and encouragement should not rest solely on the executive director's shoulders.

To bridge this gap, organizations must actively support board chairs in defining their tenure goals and provide continuous assessment as they adapt to evolving organizational needs. Executive directors play a crucial role in setting positive expectations for success, while regular evaluations of board chair performance are essential. Encouraging board chairs to conduct rudimentary self-assessments of their progress toward goals can foster confidence and promote growth, especially when coupled with constructive feedback from the organization. These self-evaluations enable board chairs to reflect on their experiences and skills in driving governance progress. Additionally, practical evaluations conducted in collaboration with governing partners can offer timely feedback to maintain board chair motivation and drive towards goal attainment, despite their limited tenure in the role. There are a lot of resources out there, and I have links on my website that you can access which you might find useful in this process.

Grab a cup of coffee and COMMUNICATE!

Beyond the essential meetings you'll schedule (hint hint: at least once each month), consider jumpstarting your relationship with a social activity. Whether it's a leisurely walk, a casual glass of wine, or a shared dinner outing, make time early on to connect on a personal level. Although the tenure may be brief, the impact is substantial, and the most successful partnerships stem from a foundation of trust and mutual understanding. Research demonstrates that social connections foster stronger relationships and enhance communication, particularly during challenging moments in the boardroom. Be open, be transparent about your work, and remember that you're both there because you WANT to be there!

Final Thoughts

When onboarding a nonprofit board chair, the path to success is illuminated by a clear understanding of the organizational culture, ongoing support, and effective communication. As I've shared throughout this book, the relationship between the executive director and the board chair sets the tone for the *entire* organization. The board chair's success is a continuous effort fueled by information, empowerment, encouragement, and support. By providing a comprehensive "backpack" of essential information and resources, organizations can equip their board chairs for success from the outset and ensure the knowledge stays with the role, term after term. Moreover, fostering a culture of transparency, trust, and inclusivity is paramount to building strong partnerships and effective governance structures.

By demystifying the role of the board chair and establishing clear expectations for involvement and accountability, you can ensure a smooth transition and strong pipeline of governing leader. Drawing from the insights shared by board chairs in my study, it was evident that a personalized approach to onboarding, supported by ongoing communication and feedback, is essential to fostering a sense of efficacy and empowerment in the board chair role. The journey of onboarding a nonprofit board chair is not just about orientation— it's about cultivating a dynamic partnership grounded in shared values, mutual respect, and a commitment to the organization's mission. Through thoughtful planning and targeted support, you can set your board chair up for success and pave the way for impactful governance and mission-driven leadership year after year. My hope is that this blueprint for successful onboarding helps create efficiencies for you and your team so when the time comes and board chair term limits are up at your nonprofit, it's easier for you to fill the seat!

About the Author

Dr. Kate Shilvock is a nonprofit executive, governance expert, and seasoned fundraiser, as well as an avid community volunteer with 25 years of proven servant-leadership success in established and emerging cultural, education, and community services nonprofits. She is an agent for change and her wealth of experience ranges from streamlining organizational processes and procedures through iterative and efficient program management, to inspiring teams towards exponential fundraising growth. Dr. Shilvock is passionate about helping nonprofit organizations embody their core values by effective operationalization of their mission and vision throughout the community, while building consensus through inclusive and equitable leadership. Kate holds a Doctorate in Organizational Change and Leadership from the University of Southern California where her national study identified nonprofit board chair onboarding practices for effective governance. She holds a BA in Sociology from Wake Forest University, and an MA in Nonprofit Administration from the University of San Francisco where her work focused on how small nonprofit organizations differentiate themselves in crowded urban markets. Dr. Shilvock is currently the executive director of an environmental conservation nonprofit, and lives in the San Francisco Bay Area with her husband and their two wonderful kids.